INNOVATORS

Urban Entrepreneur: Innovators

Scobre Educational
2255 Calle Clara
La Jolla, CA 92037

Scobre Operations & Administration
42982 Osgood Road
Fremont, CA 94539

www.scobre.com
info@scobre.com

Scobre Educational publications may be purchased for educational, business, or sales promotional use.

Cover and layout design by Jana Ramsay
Copyedited by Susan Sylvia
Some photos by Getty Images

ISBN: 978-1-61570-518-4

TABLE OF CONTENTS

Chapter 1
A Series of Remarkable Innovations

If you're like most people, there are probably a lot of things you take for granted. We have sneakers so we don't have to walk around barefoot all day. We have clothes so we don't have to walk around naked. At school, we'd rather sit at a desk than on the floor.

Most of us don't think about things after we buy them. Once they become part of our lives, we assume that they are normal and necessary. But they wouldn't even exist if it weren't for innovators. These are the people who come up with ideas to make our lives easier and more enjoyable.

Once a product has been invented, other people usually come along and improve upon it. In some cases, they will take a product and come up with a new and different use for it. This is known as innovation.

Here's a good example of innovation. First, Thomas Edison invented the electric light bulb in 1879.

Thomas Edison with one of his many inventions: the light bulb.

An invention is something brand new. It's a product that didn't exist until someone created it. An innovation is a new *use* for that product.

More than 20 years later, a man named Conrad Hubert came up with an innovation to this product – the flashlight. If there hadn't been electric light in the first place, the flashlight wouldn't have come along either.

Let's check out a more modern example. A long time ago, people only used to listen to music at home. They would listen on a record player or on the radio. Then there was a remarkable series of innovations. For the first time ever, people were able to take their music with them anywhere they went. There were cassette and CD players in cars, and Walkmans and boom boxes to take to the gym or beach.

The next innovation was even more important. As you can probably guess, it was the iPod. This little device makes it easy for anyone to carry around thousands of songs wherever they go. In addition to music, we now use our iPods to watch videos, TV shows, and movies.

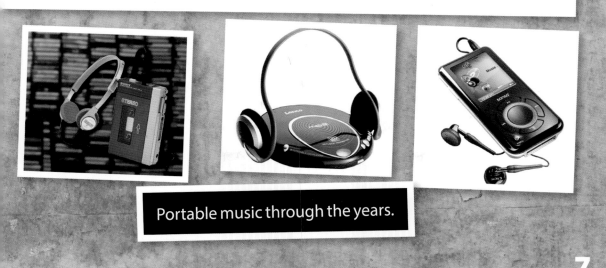

Portable music through the years.

Chapter 2
That Could Be You

When it comes to innovation, maybe nothing has been improved upon more than video games. These days, video games let us sing, play sports, or wander through make-believe worlds. That's only the beginning. We can do almost anything simply by flipping on a Wii, X-box, or Play Station.

This is very important to the world of big business. The video game

industry rakes in more than thirty billion dollars every year. This is because of innovations designed after video games were invented.

Many people have contributed to the development of video games. If it wasn't for a tech whiz named Jerry Lawson, they might have been very different than they are today.

Jerry was motivated to work hard from a very young age. When he was in first grade, he found a photo of the famous African-American inventor George Washington Carver. His teacher looked right at him.

"Jerry," the teacher said, "that could be you."

George Washington Carver created over 100 products out of peanuts, including library paste, cloth dye, and candy.

Jerry never forgot this encouragement. His teacher's comment inspired him. It made him realize that he could do anything he wanted. In the early 1970s, after Jerry was done with school, he worked in Silicon Valley. In those days, very few African-American engineers could be found in Silicon Valley, or in the technology field at all. Luckily, Jerry helped to change all of that.

Silicon Valley is an area in Northern California. It's known for being home to many big technology companies, such as Apple, Google, and Ebay.

Jerry was the leader of a team of engineers and developers working on cartridge-based video game consoles. In the mid-1970s, Jerry developed the first video-game console system designed for home use. Up until then, video game consoles were pre-programmed by

A modern cartridge-based video game console.

companies, and each console could only play one game. But Jerry's invention allowed players to simply switch small cartridges to play different games. His system was known as the "Fairchild Channel F." It opened the door for the type of systems we enjoy today.

Jerry's invention: The Fairchild Channel F

One person who is probably very grateful for Jerry's invention of the cartridge-based gaming system is Ethan Nichols, an app developer. We all know what an "app" is – these are special tools, games, and

The name, "app" is short for "application." There are more than 500,000 apps, with more being developed every day.

programs for smartphones and tablets. But what do apps have to do with cartridge-based gaming systems?

Jerry Lawson designed his video game system so that players could play more than one game on a single device. From there, it was a natural leap to apps—lots of games or programs that we use on a single smartphone or tablet. Just as the iPod was an innovation in listening to music, apps are an innovation in gaming and software development.

Many of them are fun and useful.

Many apps are created by individuals, not by big companies. They get sold through websites or through iTunes. Lots of them are free, and others sell for as little as 99 cents. That may not sound like a lot, but you'd be surprised to hear how profitable a cheap app can be.

Ethan Nicholas is an urban entrepreneur with a true story of success. Just a few years ago, Ethan became interested in creating an app for the iPhone. His idea was a video game. Every day, after coming home from work, he would spend hours developing the new game. He named it iShoot. The game became popular and Ethan has made more than $1 million as a result.

Ethan Nicolas is an innovator and an entrepreneur all rolled into one. He's certainly not alone. There will be many other opportunities available in the future. As they come online, sharp entrepreneurs will be ready to take advantage of them and make a pile of money.

Chapter 3
The Entrepreneurial Spirit of America

Innovators don't just improve on complicated technology like video game consoles or apps. Sometimes it's a simple thing—like improving the water gun.

It's a typical summer day in the big city. Blazing hot outside, over 90 degrees. Young people are looking for fun things to do so they can cool off.

Out-of-control water fights are always great. In some city neighborhoods, they are almost mandatory. Water balloons get blasted from

A summer standoff with Super Soakers.

across the street. Buckets of water are bombed from balconies. Fire hydrants are unscrewed (with appropriate permission, of course), spraying water 30 feet in the air.

The end of the water fight is the most fun, when everybody is armed with a Super Soaker. This cool toy holds two quarts of water, and it can blast up to 25 feet. The water fight has turned into an all-out water-gun battle. Everyone is having a great time – and nobody will leave dry.

You've probably never wondered how a product like the Super Soaker could be so profitable – it is obviously popular now, but before it was invented, who could have come up with an idea like that? His name was Lonnie Johnson, and he loved inventing new stuff.

Lonnie was from Marietta, Georgia, and attended an all-black high school called Williamson. It was the 1960s

A demonstration against school segregation in 1962.

and segregation was everywhere. When he was 18 years old, Lonnie invented a remote control robot. He named it Linex, and his invention won first place in a national science competition. Thanks to Lonnie's talent and perseverance, he was able to overcome any challenges he faced.

After graduating from college, Lonnie had many important jobs. He even worked for NASA (the National Aeronautics and Space Administration). NASA is an agency of the United States that is responsible for many things, including space travel.

Lonnie Johnson loved inventing and innovating. One of his greatest creations was the Super Soaker. One day he was working on a heat pump at his home. He connected the pump to the faucet in his bathroom. All of a sudden, water shot out very quickly. Lonnie's first thought was that it would make an excellent water gun.Lonnie was right about how popular his new water gun would be. The Super Soaker was introduced to the general public in 1991. This fun and innovative toy sold well right from the beginning. By now, Super Soakers have made over $1 billion in profit worldwide.

How many of us would ever look at the Super Soaker and realize how profitable it would be? This simple and fun toy shows us that even small things can become very important. That's how entrepreneurs look at things. It's not easy to invent something from scratch. It's also very difficult to

Kids look at a toy and decide if it will be fun. Adults care mostly about the price, and whether a product is safe. What about the entrepreneur? They are the ones who get a business or an invention off the ground. He or she is always wondering the same thing: Will this new idea be popular? How can I make money with this great invention? Most importantly, *how will my product improve the world?*

It is easy to take certain innovations for granted. How many people know that the modern clock was invented by a black man named Benjamin Banneker, way back in 1753?

innovate a better or newer version of an existing product. But if someone wants to do either of those things, it's also important to understand how to make money from it. This is the entrepreneurial spirit of America.

In big cities all across this country, urban entrepreneurs are looking for the next big thing. Throughout history, even during difficult times, Americans from all walks of life continue to innovate. We have developed innovations in everything from toys and computers, to refrigerators and clocks. It's important to remember that a great idea can be successful no matter who comes up with it.

Through good times and bad times, creative entrepreneurs are always coming up with ideas. Even during the Great Depression of the 1930s, cool things were being invented. One of them was the chocolate chip cookie! Another was the best-selling board game of all time – Monopoly.

Chapter 4
Business and Creativity

When a product is invented or innovated, it doesn't magically end up at your school or in your home. Somebody has to buy it. That means people have to like (or need) something. They have to make the decision to spend money on it. There are so many different products out there. So what actually influences people to choose one thing over another?

The answer is simple: advertising, marketing, promotion, and publicity. These words all add up to the same thing:

They spread the word about your product. On TV, there are commercials. If you pick up any newspaper or magazine, there are tons of ads. We've all seen huge billboards in big cities—even on the sides of buses, or sidewalk benches. Then, of course, there's the internet. On almost every website you visit, there are pop-ups, banners, text ads – you name it. It's all about advertising. There's almost no way to escape it.

Times Square in New York City is covered with advertising.

It takes time, effort, and money to invent a new product, or open a business. But despite the hard work, there's a reason people want to get in the mix: the possibility of making a big profit. These urban entrepreneurs with big dreams are the cornerstones of business.

Lonnie Johnson believed that his new water gun could be an extremely popular toy. He was right, but he didn't get paid right away. It took almost ten years until the Super Soaker was ready to be sold in stores. Then, once it finally hit the store shelves, people needed to find out about it. That's where marketing comes in.

However, advertising doesn't always

work. Sometimes there is hype about a new invention, but it falls flat. Take Apple, for example. Whenever Apple has something new coming out, it's a reason to celebrate. Steve Jobs (who passed away in 2011) was like a rock star in the world of technology.

Years ago, Apple had a new product coming out. This new device was supposed to be different than everything else on the market. It promised to be very cool and make your life easier and more fun. And, oh yeah, it was really expensive. But what was the product? The iPhone? Or maybe the iPad? Actually, this was the hype surrounding a device Apple brought out in 1993. It was known as the Newton.

You've probably never heard of the Newton. It was a "PDA" (Personal Digital Assistant). It was a portable device that looked like a tablet. It could do things like take notes and store

gty.im/
90766345

Science & Society
Picture Library

Apple's Newton

The Newton was named after Sir Isaac Newton. This great thinker famously developed a theory about gravity after watching an apple fall from a tree.

phone numbers. Some people might say it was like the iPad of the early 1990s. Except there was one difference: the iPad was a success from day one. The Newton, on the other hand, was a total bust.

Apple hyped the Newton big-time, but that didn't matter. It failed for many reasons. To start with, it was very expensive, and it didn't work very well.

It simply didn't deliver on its promise to improve peoples' lives. As a matter of fact, it was such a disappointment that people mocked it.

There's an important lesson here. Even though things don't always work out, keep at it. Never give up. People like Steve Jobs never did. He was a true entrepreneur and innovator. He had more than 300 patents in his own name. The Newton may have failed, but he didn't let that stop him. Good thing, too, because he went on to rule the technology world.

And Steve Jobs wasn't the only one. Urban entrepreneurs are people who are right in the middle of things. Maybe it's because they look at the world through a different set of eyes than most of us. They have a combination of business sense and creativity. They figure out how to make money in ways that the average person doesn't.

Want to hear an ironic story? After Mr. Jobs passed away, somebody tweeted, "who is Steve Jobs?" Right below, it said, "sent from my iPhone."

The television set was one of the greatest inventions in history. But it wasn't until the 1950s that TVs became common household items. Times were good, and average people could afford to buy a TV. After that, it was all about

Televisions sure have changed a lot over the years!

innovation—new shows, new ideas, and new TV networks.

Fast forward to January, 1980. For anyone interested in business, that was an important time. It's still pretty important today—that is, if you enjoy shows like 106 & Park, MoNique, the Soul Train Awards, and the Hip Hop Awards, all provided by BET – Black Entertainment TV.

Back in 1980, nobody could have predicted such great success for BET. It struggled for a long time, and started out as a very small network. It produced only a couple of hours of content a day. Very few people were watching.

But finally, after BET started showing a lot of music videos, things began to turn around. They don't focus only on music videos anymore, but BET remains a very popular network. It's watched by hundreds of thousands of people every day.

BET was the brainchild of a very ambitious man. He had an idea to create

Music videos are fun to watch, and a great way for artists to promote their songs. They're not cheap to produce, though. The most expensive video of all time is "Scream," by Michael Jackson in 1995. It's been viewed more than 20 million times on YouTube.

programming for African-Americans. His name is Robert "Bob" Johnson.

Bob was born in Hickory, Mississippi, in 1946. He was one of 10 brothers and sisters. He and his family eventually moved to Freeport, Illinois. That's where young Bob got his first taste of the working world. He delivered newspapers before he was even a teenager. Later on, he was proud

Robert Johnson (left) attends BET's 25th anniversary celebration.

to be the first member of his family to graduate from college.

In the 1970s, it dawned on Bob that there wasn't a lot of diversity on TV. There weren't many shows for him, his friends, and their community. Instead of just hoping for more shows like that, Bob did something about it. *I'm going to invent a network for black people.* So he raised the money he needed to get started. Once things eventually got rolling, BET was a huge success, and it branched out. Bob moved his company into the business of magazines, books, and even additional TV channels.

Bob has a lot to be proud of. In 2003, Mr. Johnson became the main owner of the NBA's Charlotte Bobcats. A couple years later, Michael Jordan joined him and became a part-owner.

In the year 2000, Bob sold BET to a huge media company called Viacom. Just twenty years earlier, it had taken an investment of about a half-million dollars to get BET off the ground. But when Mr. Johnson sold BET to Viacom, the price tag was three billion dollars.

Some kids think that unless they end up working in entertainment or sports, they won't be successful. Nothing could be further from the truth. There are urban entrepreneurs making money in your city right now. They are finding success in many different ways, because they understand that opportunity is all around us.

Think about Bob Johnson. He has a bigger bank account than any athlete, and Bob did it the old fashioned way. He went to school, worked hard, had a great idea, and succeeded in making that idea into a reality. Your journey could be the same – and it starts right now.

Are you ready?